HISTORY CORNER

Ancient Egyptians

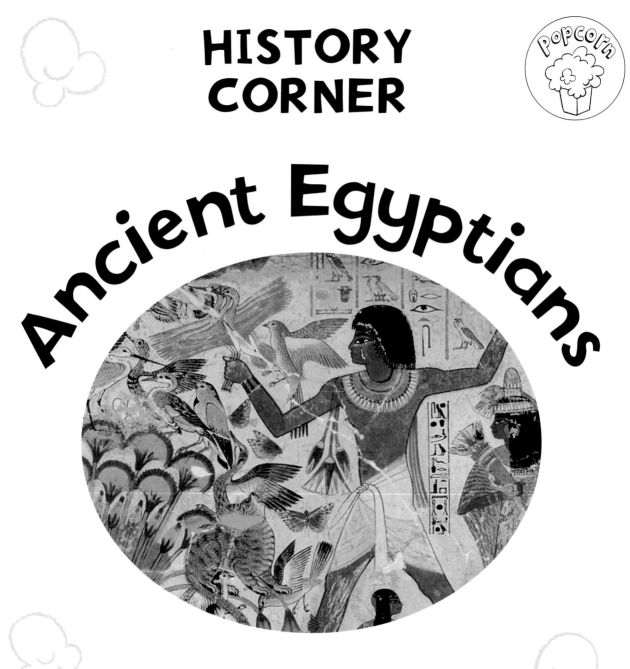

Alice Harman

WAYLAND

Explore the world with **Popcorn -** your complete first non-fiction library.

Look out for more titles in the Popcorn range. All books have the same format of simple text and striking images. Text is carefully matched to the pictures to help readers to identify and understand key vocabulary.
www.waylandbooks.co.uk/popcorn

First published in 2012 by Wayland
Copyright © Wayland 2012

Wayland
Hachette Children's Books
338 Euston Road
London NW1 3BH

Wayland Australia
Level 17/207 Kent Street
Sydney NSW 2000

Produced for Wayland by
White-Thomson Publishing Ltd
www.wtpub.co.uk
+44 (0)843 208 7460

Editor: Alice Harman
Designer: Clare Nicholas
Picture researcher: Alice Harman
Series consultant: Kate Ruttle
Design concept: Paul Cherrill

British Library Cataloguing in Publication Data
Harman, Alice.
   Ancient Egyptians. -- (History corner)(Popcorn)
   1. Egypt--History--To 322 B.C.--Juvenile literature.
   2. Egypt--Civilization--To 332 B.C--Juvenile literature.
   I. Title II. Series
   932'.01-dc23

   ISBN: 978 0 7502 6734 2

Wayland is a division of Hachette Children's Books,
an Hachette UK company.
www.hachette.co.uk

Printed and bound in China

Picture/illustration credits:
Alamy: The Art Archive 9; Peter Bull 23; Stefan Chabluk 4; Corbis: Wener Forman 11; Gianni Dagli Orti 15; Getty: The Bridgeman Art Library front cover; De Agostini 13; Shutterstock: John Said 16; Nicole Gordine 22; Werner Forman: British Museum 5; British Museum 10; E.Strouhal 12; British Museum 14; Wikimedia: Ricardo Liberato 6; Bjørn Christian Tørrissen 7; Rama and Jeff Dahl 8; John Campana 17; 18; The Yorck Project 18; Stormnight 18; BrokenSphere 19; The Yorck Project 20; 21.

Every effort has been made to clear copyright. Should there be any inadvertent omission, please apply to the publisher for rectification.

 Contents

Who were the ancient Egyptians?

The ancient Egyptians lived in Egypt, in the area shown on this map. They built their towns close to the River Nile.

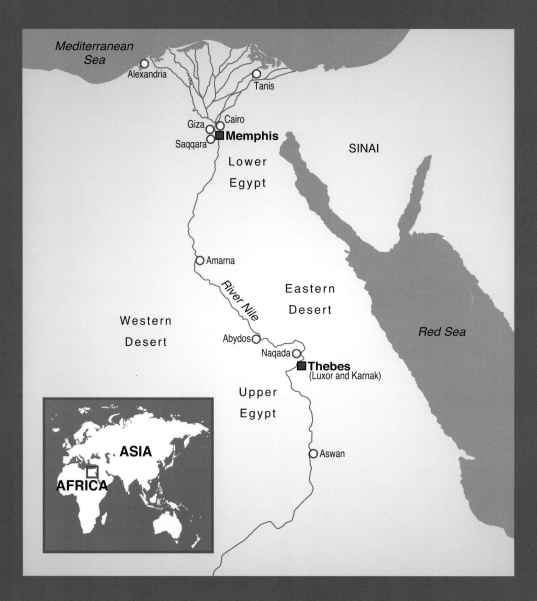

Mediterranean Sea

Alexandria

Tanis

Giza Cairo

Saqqara ■ **Memphis**

L o w e r

E g y p t

SINAI

Amarna

River Nile

Eastern

Desert

Western

Desert

Abydos

Naqada

Red Sea

■ **Thebes**
(Luxor and Karnak)

U p p e r

E g y p t

Aswan

ASIA

AFRICA

The ancient Egyptians
lived between 5,000 and
2,000 years ago.

We can find out
about how the
ancient Egyptians
lived by looking
at the objects
they made.

The pharaohs

The kings and queens that ruled over ancient Egypt were called pharaohs. Pharaohs were very rich and powerful.

There were around ten female pharaohs, including Cleopatra, the last pharaoh.

The pyramids of Giza were built as tombs for the pharaohs Khufu, Khafre and Menkaure.

One of the most famous pharaohs is Tutankhamun. He became king at the age of ten and died when he was about 18 years old.

This gold mask is one of many treasures found in the tomb of Tutankhamun.

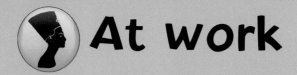# At work

Most ancient Egyptians could not read or write. Scribes were men whose job was to write things down for people. Ancient Egyptian writing is called hieroglyphics.

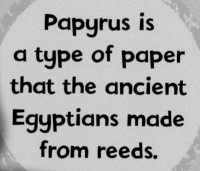

Papyrus is a type of paper that the ancient Egyptians made from reeds.

Most ancient Egyptian men were farmers. They grew crops and kept animals. Children in poorer families also often worked on farms.

Paintings on the walls of ancient Egyptian tombs show farmers working in the fields.

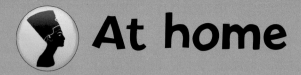

At home

Most ancient Egyptian families lived in small mud or clay houses in towns or villages. Women normally worked in the home and looked after the children.

Clay models show that most houses had flat roofs, where families sat in the evening.

Rich families lived in large houses called villas. A villa had lots of rooms and gardens. There was sometimes a swimming pool and a small chapel.

Wall paintings show many servants and slaves working in villas.

 Children

Children had shaved heads, except for one thick piece of hair in a plait. Around the age of 13, this piece of hair was cut off. This meant the child had become an adult.

Princes held their hair in place with a band of gold and jewels.

Most children did not go to school. Boys were taught how to do the same work as their father. Girls learned how to cook, clean and take care of younger children.

Paintings show children helping adults with work, such as picking grapes from the trees.

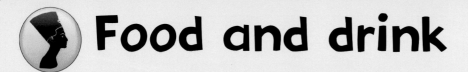

Food and drink

Ancient Egyptians used the River Nile for collecting water, hunting and fishing. The wet soil on the riverbank was also good for growing crops.

This man is hunting wild birds with his cat, while his wife and daughter watch.

Women in ancient Egypt made flour by grinding grains between two stones. They mixed this flour with milk and salt to make bread.

This wooden model shows servants working together in the kitchen.

Kings and queens ate bread flavoured with fruit, spices and honey.

Clothes and jewellery

Both rich and poor people wore clothes made of light, white cloth. These kept them cool in the hot weather. Children often didn't wear any clothes at all.

Men wore a type of skirt around their waist, and most women wore simple dresses.

Ancient Egyptian men and women wore jewellery such as necklaces, bracelets and earrings. Jewellery was often made from solid gold.

A pectoral was worn on the chest, often at the end of a long necklace.

This gold pectoral contains 372 pieces of coloured precious stones.

turquoise

lapis lazuli

garnet

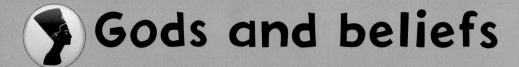

Gods and beliefs

People in ancient Egypt believed in more than 2,000 gods and goddesses. They tried to keep them happy with prayers and gifts. Gods were often shown with animal heads.

Re, the sun god, had the head of a falcon.

The ancient Egyptians thought people began another life after they died. A dead person's body was specially prepared and wrapped in cloth, to make it into a mummy.

The mummy was put in a sarcophagus, a coffin often painted with magic spells and prayers.

When poor people died, they were buried in the sand.

Fun and leisure

Senet was a very popular board game in ancient Egypt. Both rich and poor people played it. Senet is one of the oldest board games in the world.

Queen Nefertari, wife of the pharaoh Rameses II, is shown playing senet in this wall painting.

The ancient Egyptians celebrated at parties and religious festivals with music and dance. Pictures often show musicians playing harps and pipes.

Musicians and dancers were often women, and they mostly performed in groups of two or three.

Hand clapping was a big part of ancient Egyptian music.

Write in hieroglyphs

The ancient Egyptians wrote using pictures called hieroglyphs. There were more than 700 different hieroglyphs. Some pictures stood for whole words. Other words were made by using different hieroglyphs together.

This alphabet shows how Egyptian hieroglyphs match up with the letters that we use today.

Try to write your name in hieroglyphs!

Make a model pyramid

You will need:
· plain white paper
· colouring pencils
· pencil · black pen
· scissors · ruler
· sticky tape

Pyramids were built as tombs for some ancient Egyptian pharaohs. There are more than 130 pyramids in Egypt, but the most famous ones are in Giza. It took thousands of people many years to build the biggest pyramids.

1. Copy this template, using a ruler and pencil. Cut out the shape.

2. Colour in your pyramid with a yellow colouring pencil. Draw on a brick pattern with a brown colouring pencil. Draw hieroglyphs on the pyramid sides with a black pen.

3. Fold the triangles upwards, so they form a pyramid. Use sticky tape to stick the edges of the triangles together.

Visit our website to download larger, printable templates for this project.

www.waylandbooks.co.uk/popcorn

23

Glossary

chapel a small church

coffin a box that holds the body of a dead person

crops plants grown for food, for people or animals

falcon a bird that catches and eats smaller birds

grain the seed of a plant such as wheat or barley

harp a triangle-shaped musical instrument with strings that a person plucks with both hands

pipes a musical instrument that the player blows into with their mouth

reeds plants with long, thin stems that grow near water

servant a person who works in someone else's house, cooking, cleaning or looking after the home in other ways

tomb a grave, where someone's body is put when they die

Index

EXPLORE THE WORLD WITH THE POPCORN NON-FICTION LIBRARY!

- Develops children's knowledge and understanding of the world by covering a wide range of topics in a fun, colourful and engaging way
- Simple sentence structure builds readers' confidence
- Text checked by an experienced literacy consultant and primary deputy-head teacher
- Closely matched pictures and text enable children to decode words
- Includes a cross-curricular activity in the back of each book

WATCH OUT! — Near Water — Honor Head

HISTORY CORNER — The Great Fire of London — Jenny Powell

SCIENCE CORNER — Sound and Hearing — Angela Royston

FAMILIES — My Mum — Katie Dicker

GOOD FOOD — Vegetables — Julia Adams

PEOPLE WHO HELP US — Police — Honor Head

PEOPLE WHO HELP US — Firefighters — Honor Head

GEOGRAPHY CORNER — Rainforests — Saranne Taylor

A YEAR OF FESTIVALS — Muslim Festivals — Honor Head

HISTORY CORNER — The Gunpowder Plot — Jenny Powell

IN SPACE — Planets — Chris Oxlade

SEASONS — Winter — Kay Barnham

FREE DOWNLOADS!

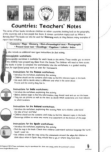

OVER 50 TITLES TO CHOOSE FROM!

- Written by an experienced teacher
- Learning objectives clearly marked
- Provides information on where the books fit into the curriculum
- Photocopiable so pupils can take them home

www.waylandbooks.co.uk/downloads